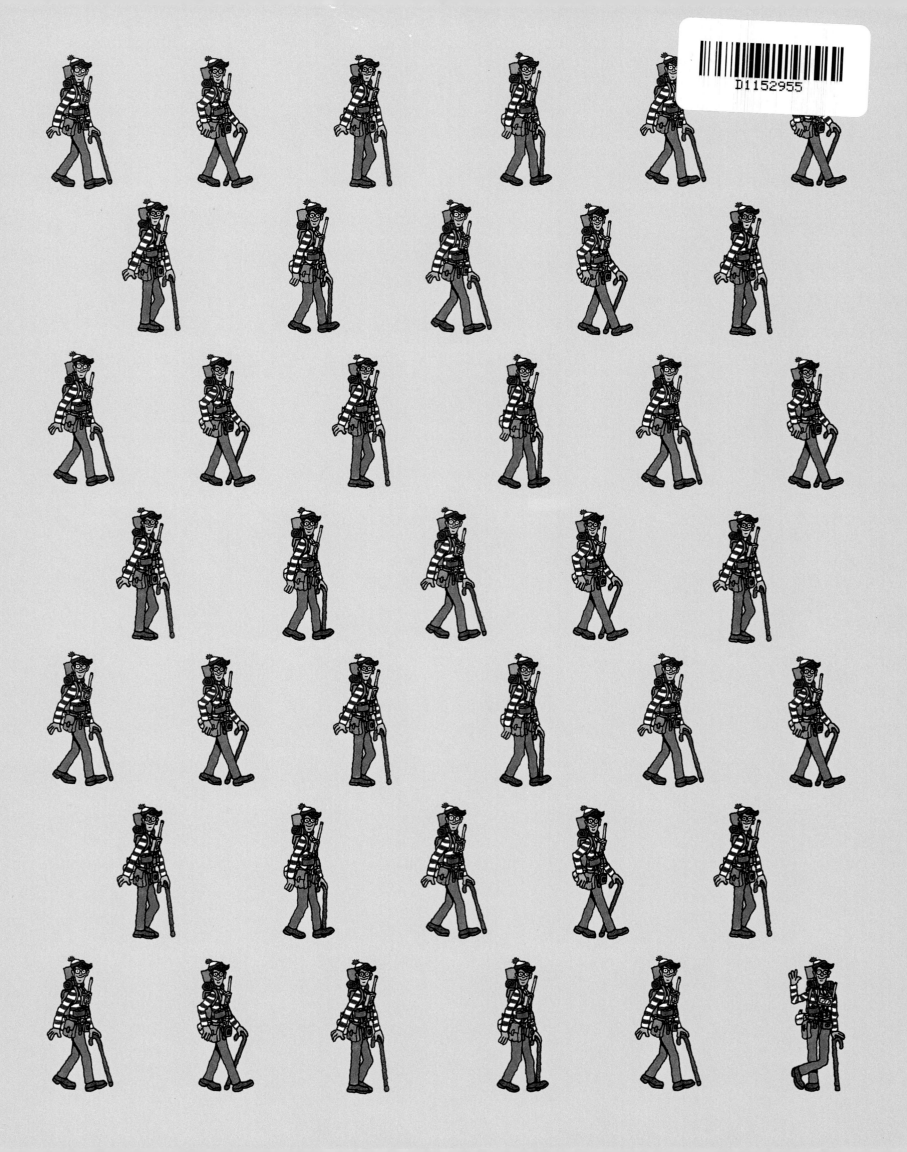

For Wally

First published 1987 by Walker Books Ltd
87 Vauxhall Walk, London SE11 5HJ

This edition published for The Book People

2 4 6 8 10 9 7 5 3 1

© 1987, 1997, 2007, 2011 Martin Handford

The right of Martin Handford to be identified as author/illustrator
of this work has been asserted by him in accordance with the
Copyright, Designs and Patents Act 1988.

This book has been typeset in Wallyfont

Printed in China

British Library Cataloguing in Publication Data:
a catalogue record for this book
is available from the British Library.

ISBN 978-1-4063-5388-4

www.walker.co.uk

WHERE'S WALLY?

MARTIN HANDFORD

DELUXE EDITION

WALKER BOOKS
AND SUBSIDIARIES

LONDON • BOSTON • SYDNEY • AUCKLAND

CHECKLIST: IN TOWN

- [ ] A dog on a roof
- [ ] A man on a fountain
- [ ] A man about to trip over a dog's lead
- [ ] A car crash
- [ ] A keen barber
- [ ] People in a street, watching television
- [ ] A puncture caused by an arrow
- [ ] A tearful tune
- [ ] A boy attacked by a plant
- [ ] Three sandwiches
- [ ] Eight buckets

- [ ] A waiter who isn't concentrating
- [ ] Two firemen waving at each other
- [ ] A face on a wall
- [ ] A man coming out of a man hole
- [ ] A man feeding birds
- [ ] Someone wearing a pair of yellow boots
- [ ] Two people reading newspapers
- [ ] Seven ladders and ten striped canopies

ONE MORE THING!

On every flap is a collection of special souvenir stamps of the people and animals Wally has met on his travels. Can you find the pictures on the stamps in each relevant scene? First class!

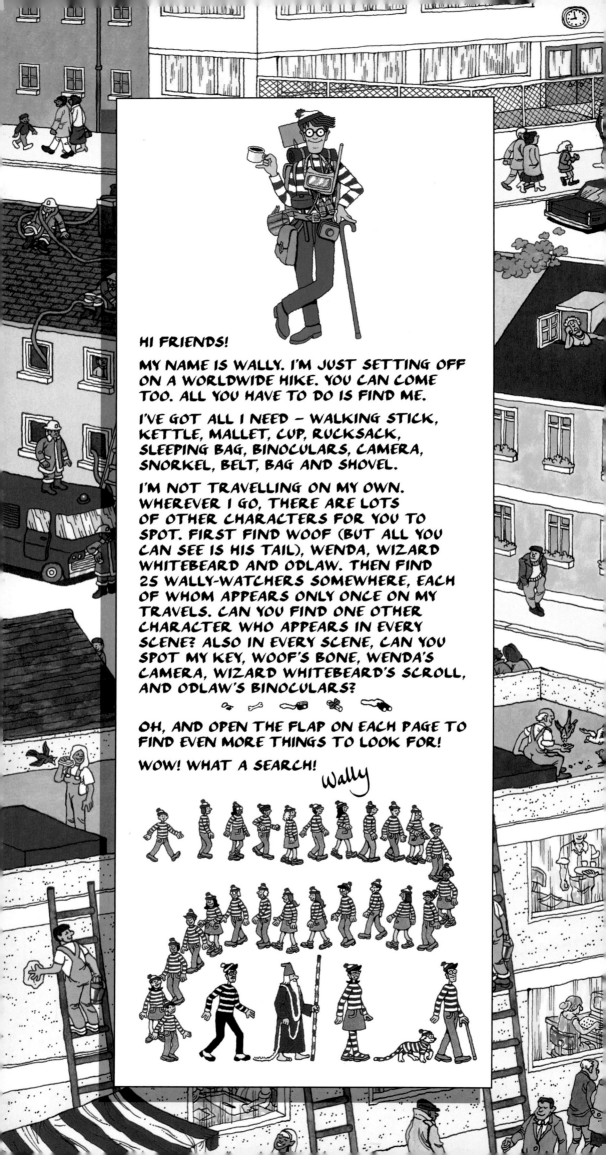

HI FRIENDS!

MY NAME IS WALLY. I'M JUST SETTING OFF ON A WORLDWIDE HIKE. YOU CAN COME TOO. ALL YOU HAVE TO DO IS FIND ME.

I'VE GOT ALL I NEED – WALKING STICK, KETTLE, MALLET, CUP, RUCKSACK, SLEEPING BAG, BINOCULARS, CAMERA, SNORKEL, BELT, BAG AND SHOVEL.

I'M NOT TRAVELLING ON MY OWN. WHEREVER I GO, THERE ARE LOTS OF OTHER CHARACTERS FOR YOU TO SPOT. FIRST FIND WOOF (BUT ALL YOU CAN SEE IS HIS TAIL), WENDA, WIZARD WHITEBEARD AND ODLAW. THEN FIND 25 WALLY-WATCHERS SOMEWHERE, EACH OF WHOM APPEARS ONLY ONCE ON MY TRAVELS. CAN YOU FIND ONE OTHER CHARACTER WHO APPEARS IN EVERY SCENE? ALSO IN EVERY SCENE, CAN YOU SPOT MY KEY, WOOF'S BONE, WENDA'S CAMERA, WIZARD WHITEBEARD'S SCROLL, AND ODLAW'S BINOCULARS?

OH, AND OPEN THE FLAP ON EACH PAGE TO FIND EVEN MORE THINGS TO LOOK FOR!

WOW! WHAT A SEARCH!

Wally

CHECKLIST: ON THE BEACH

- A dog and its owners wearing sunglasses
- A man who is overdressed
- A muscular medallion man
- A cross looking human stepping stone
- A water skier
- A stripy photographer
- A punctured lilo
- A donkey who likes ice cream
- A man being squashed
- A punctured beach ball
- A human pyramid
- A muscleman next to two half musclemen
- Three people reading newspapers
- A cowboy
- A human donkey
- A red ball
- Nine children holding spades
- Four giant fish
- A radio
- A red lilo

- Age and beauty
- Two red and yellow umbrellas
- Two men with vests, one without
- A show-off with sandcastles
- Three men wearing red caps and sunglasses
- Someone wearing braces
- A cream coloured dog
- Three protruding tongues
- Two oddly fitting hats
- Eight children holding ice creams
- Five sprinters
- A towel with a hole in it
- A punctured hovercraft
- A boy who's not allowed any ice cream
- Two caps with extra long peaks
- A polite man raising his hat to a lady
- Four chairs

CHECKLIST: SKI SLOPES

- [ ] A man reading on a roof
- [ ] A flying skier
- [ ] A runaway skier
- [ ] A backward skier
- [ ] A portrait in snow
- [ ] An illegal fisherman
- [ ] Five people wearing stripy scarves
- [ ] Snow about to fall on two laughing men
- [ ] Three skiers who have hit trees
- [ ] An Alpine horn
- [ ] Two broken flagpoles
- [ ] A flag collector
- [ ] Four people in yellow-hooded tops
- [ ] A skier up a tree
- [ ] One skier with four skis
- [ ] A pair of empty skates
- [ ] A skiing snowman
- [ ] A parachute

- [ ] A water skier on snow
- [ ] A Yeti
- [ ] Two skiing reindeer
- [ ] A roof jumper
- [ ] Someone crashing through five skiers
- [ ] Three skiers sitting down
- [ ] A tree which is wider at the top
- [ ] Someone with different coloured ski boots
- [ ] Ski goggles worn back to front

CHECKLIST: CAMP SITE

- [ ] A bull in a hedge
- [ ] Bull horns
- [ ] A shark in a canal
- [ ] A bull seeing red
- [ ] A careless kick
- [ ] Tea in a lap
- [ ] A low bridge
- [ ] A person knocked over by a mallet
- [ ] A man surprised undressing
- [ ] A bicycle tyre about to be punctured
- [ ] Six dogs
- [ ] A scarecrow that doesn't work
- [ ] A wigwam
- [ ] Large biceps
- [ ] Three campers with very long beards
- [ ] A lady holding a fan
- [ ] Eight fish
- [ ] An artist

- [ ] A collapsed tent
- [ ] A smoking barbecue
- [ ] A fisherman catching old boots
- [ ] A winning penny-farthing
- [ ] A boy scout making fire
- [ ] A roller hiker
- [ ] A man blowing up a dinghy
- [ ] Thirsty walkers
- [ ] Runners on the road
- [ ] A bull chasing two people
- [ ] Two gates
- [ ] A camper's butler
- [ ] Welcome water running from a tap
- [ ] Animals posing for photographs
- [ ] A romantic foursome

CHECKLIST: THE RAILWAY STATION

- Someone desperately trying to lift a suitcase
- Four shovels and five spades
- A trolley carrying five suitcases
- People being knocked over by a door
- A man about to step on a ball
- Three different times at the same time
- A wheelbarrow pram
- A face on a train
- Five people reading one newspaper
- Someone in a white suit with a brown case
- A show-off with a suitcase
- Someone tripping over a dog
- The contents of two suitcases spilling over the ground
- Two men wearing stripy ties
- Five benches

- A smoking train
- A squeeze on a bench
- A dog tearing a man's trousers
- A man sitting on a suitcase
- Two keen ticket inspectors
- Twenty cows
- A man and his luggage breaking a weighing machine
- Eleven pots of paint
- A workman's yellow helmet on the platform
- Thirty-four railway workmen

CHECKLIST: AIRPORT

- A flying saucer
- A boy sitting with the revolving luggage
- A leaking fuel pipe
- Flight controllers playing badminton
- A rocket
- A tower on top of the control tower
- Three watch smugglers
- An airport worker resting on a plane
- A forklift truck
- A wind-sock
- Someone with a bucket and spade
- Six air hostesses in light blue uniforms
- A plane with giant tail wings
- A fire engine and ten firemen
- Twelve airport workers with blue caps

- A plane that doesn't fly
- A flying Ace
- A pen and paper
- Runners on a runway
- Five men blowing up a balloon
- Two passengers wearing white hats
- Dracula
- A tractor pulling some cargo
- Another tractor pulling some farm animals
- Three childish pilots
- Eighteen airport workers with yellow caps
- Nine luggage trolleys
- A courteous security guard impressing a lady
- A suitcase falling on somebody's foot
- Four air hostesses in green uniforms

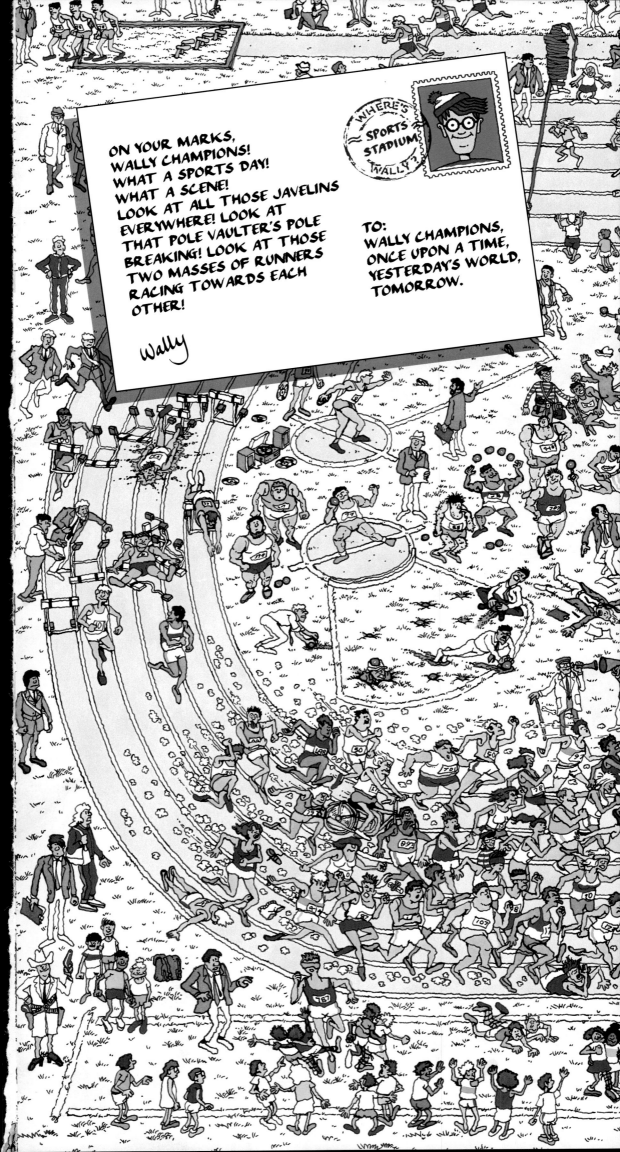

CHECKLIST: SPORTS STADIUM

- [ ] Three pairs of feet, sticking out of the sand
- [ ] A cowboy starting races
- [ ] Hopeless hurdlers
- [ ] Ten children taking part in the three-legged race
- [ ] Record discs thrown by a discus thrower
- [ ] A shot-put juggler
- [ ] An ear trumpet
- [ ] A vaulting horse
- [ ] A runner with two wheels
- [ ] A parachuting vaulter
- [ ] A Scotsman with a caber
- [ ] An elephant pulling a rope
- [ ] People being knocked over by a hammer
- [ ] Six athletes wearing red headbands
- [ ] Two duelling relay runners
- [ ] An umpire's clothes pinned down by javelins
- [ ] A long jumper with a spring in his step

- [ ] A gardener
- [ ] Three frogmen
- [ ] A runner without any shorts on
- [ ] A bed
- [ ] A bandaged boy
- [ ] A runner with four legs
- [ ] A sunken jumper
- [ ] Two athletes with stripy towels
- [ ] An umpire chasing a dog, chasing a cat, chasing a mouse
- [ ] A boy squirting water
- [ ] Twenty-two javelins
- [ ] Six really thirsty athletes
- [ ] Two colliding photographers
- [ ] Some triple triple jumpers
- [ ] Six relay race batons

CHECKLIST: MUSEUM

- [ ] A very big skeleton
- [ ] A clown squirting water
- [ ] A boy in a catapult
- [ ] A bird's nest in a woman's hair
- [ ] A popping bicep
- [ ] One circular portrait picture frame
- [ ] A knight watching television
- [ ] Picture robbers
- [ ] A toppling row of pots
- [ ] Six pictures without any people in them
- [ ] Two upside down pictures
- [ ] A museum attendant resting
- [ ] A highwayman
- [ ] Five swords
- [ ] Two drums

- [ ] A leaking watercolour
- [ ] Fighting pictures
- [ ] A king and queen
- [ ] A rude character inside a picture
- [ ] Three cavemen
- [ ] A lady wearing a red scarf
- [ ] Charioteers
- [ ] A collapsing pillar
- [ ] Three shields
- [ ] A museum attendant giving a lecture
- [ ] Someone wearing red checked trousers
- [ ] Someone wearing red boots
- [ ] Five red plumes

CHECKLIST: AT SEA

- A windsurfer
- A rubber dinghy punctured by an arrow
- A sword fight with a swordfish
- A school of whales
- Seasick sailors
- A leaking diver
- A boat which has crashed into a safety buoy
- A bathtub
- A bearded man wearing sunglasses
- A game of noughts and crosses
- Someone hit by a message in a bottle
- Five men wearing red swimming trunks
- Eleven pirate swords
- A blue paddle
- Four fishing rods

- A lucky fisherman
- Three lumberjacks
- Unlucky fishermen
- Two water skiers in a tangle
- A cowboy riding a seahorse
- Fish robbers
- A fishy photo
- Uninvited pirates climbing aboard ship
- A Chinese junk
- A wave at sea
- A man being strangled by an octopus
- An unhappy row of rowers
- A sinking boat next to a sinking island
- A boat being cut in half
- Three men wearing yellow T-shirts
- A rower holding two oars

CHECKLIST: SAFARI PARK

- [ ] Noah's Ark
- [ ] A message in a bottle
- [ ] A hippo having its teeth cleaned
- [ ] A bird's nest in an antler
- [ ] A hungry giraffe
- [ ] An ice-cream robber
- [ ] Zebras crossing a zebra crossing
- [ ] Father Christmas and a contented reindeer
- [ ] Eight birds
- [ ] A unicorn
- [ ] Fifteen safari park rangers
- [ ] A driver losing his hat
- [ ] Two animals having a snooze
- [ ] A water bowl
- [ ] A periscope

- [ ] Caged people
- [ ] A lion next to the driver in a car
- [ ] Daddy bear, mummy bear and baby bear
- [ ] Tarzan
- [ ] Lion cubs
- [ ] Two ladies with red handbags
- [ ] Two queues for the toilets
- [ ] Animals' beauty parlour
- [ ] An elephant squirting water
- [ ] A man holding a blue jacket
- [ ] Two tangled trunks
- [ ] Three banana skins

WELCOME, WALLY-WATCHERS! I SAW SOME UNFORGETTABLE SIGHTS TODAY; LOTS OF RAILS AND TABLES FULL OF COLOURFUL THINGS; SOME DEMONSTRATIONS GOING WRONG; A MAN CHECKING A WASHING MACHINE BY WASHING HIS OWN CLOTHES IN IT FIRST. PHEW! INCREDIBLE!

Wally

TO:
WALLY-WATCHERS,
OVER THE MOON,
THE WILD WEST,
NOW.

WHERE'S WALLY? DEPARTMENT STORE

CHECKLIST: DEPARTMENT STORE

- [ ] A red-suited pushchair passenger
- [ ] Someone wearing a red-and-yellow bobble hat
- [ ] A man whose boots face the wrong way
- [ ] A man with heavy shopping
- [ ] A misbehaving vacuum cleaner
- [ ] Ties that match their wearers
- [ ] Two Jack-in-the-box cases
- [ ] A pram bumping into a shopper
- [ ] A boy trying on a top hat
- [ ] Seven pairs of boots on display
- [ ] A waving glove
- [ ] A man wearing blue braces

- [ ] A man trying on a jacket that's too big
- [ ] A shopper tripping over a ball on the floor
- [ ] A girl wearing a red anorak
- [ ] A boy riding in a trolley bag
- [ ] A dangerous glove that's come alive
- [ ] Two men wearing green check trousers
- [ ] Three pairs of shoes on the floor
- [ ] A full-length mirror

CHECKLIST: FAIRGROUND

- [ ] A cannon at a rifle range
- [ ] A bumper car run wild
- [ ] Ten coloured hoops
- [ ] A one-armed bandit
- [ ] A ragdoll
- [ ] Twelve uniformed fairground staff
- [ ] A runaway fairground horse
- [ ] Thirty-one birds
- [ ] An unaware powerful thrower at the coconut shy
- [ ] Balloons flying away
- [ ] Three toy rockets
- [ ] One cat

- [ ] A haunted house
- [ ] Seven lost children and a lost dog
- [ ] A tank crash
- [ ] Twenty-three coconut shy balls
- [ ] Three clowns
- [ ] Six people with their hands up surrendering
- [ ] Three men dressed as bears
- [ ] A helter skelter pile-up
- [ ] Three scary children frightening a ghost
- [ ] One pram and one pushchair
- [ ] Twelve passengers on the land train
- [ ] Three brown dogs

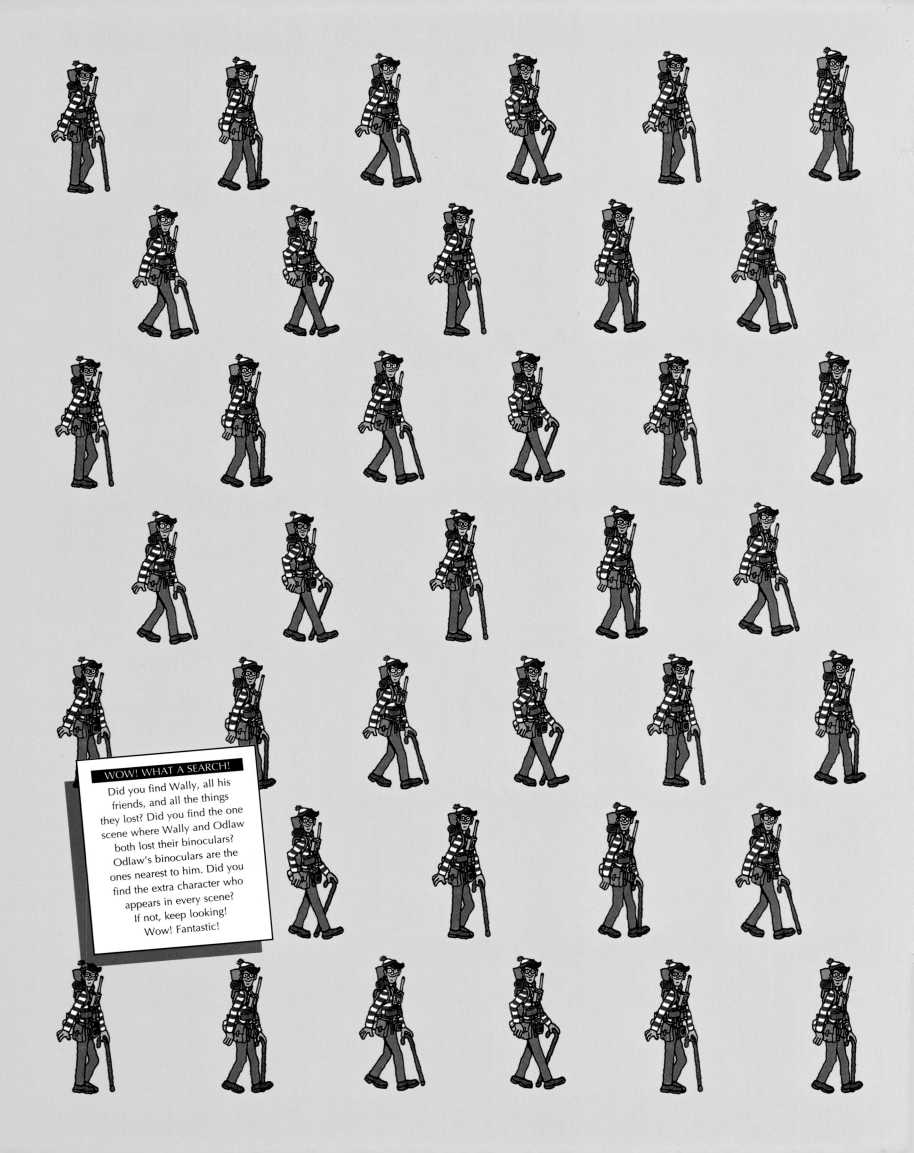

WOW! WHAT A SEARCH!

Did you find Wally, all his friends, and all the things they lost? Did you find the one scene where Wally and Odlaw both lost their binoculars? Odlaw's binoculars are the ones nearest to him. Did you find the extra character who appears in every scene? If not, keep looking! Wow! Fantastic!